BOOK REVIEW LOG BOOK

Jennifer Gilmour

Copyright © 2021 Jennifer Gilmour

ISBN: 978-1-9999647-2-6

All rights reserved. No part of this book may be reproduced or transmitted in any form or by any means, electronic or mechanical, including photocopying, recording, or by information storage or retrieval system, without the author's permission.

Hello Fellow Book Worm

I hope you enjoy using this book review log book as much as I did bringing it to life. Keep track of your next 100 reads with this book review log book. There's a handy to be read shelf, book release section, word cloud and more. I've added a notes section at the back for anything you don't want to forget about what you're reading.

Share your reading journey and let me know what you're reading by tagging me online @JenLGilmour.

Now let's get reading...

To be read

Sketch the book ends onto the shelf

To be read

Sketch the book ends onto the shelf

Book Release

Write the books you are
looking forward to coming out

JANUARY

FEBRUARY

MARCH

APRIL

MAY

JUNE

Book Release

Write the books you are looking forward to coming out

JULY	AUGUST

SEPTEMBER	OCTOBER

NOVEMBER	DECEMBER

Read 50 Books

Colour in a square when you've finished a book

1	2	3	4	5	6	7	8
9	10	11	12	13	14	15	16
17	18	19	20	21	22	23	24
25	26	27	28	29	30	31	32
33	34	35	36	37	38	39	40
41	42	43	44	45	46	47	48
49	50						

State your genre:

Word Cloud

Add words that inspire you as you read

BOOK REVIEW

Print your book cover and paste it here

Size: 2.5cm x 3cm

Title: _____

Author: _____

Date Started: _____

Date Finished: _____

Format: Physical   eBook   Audiobook

Rating: ☆ ☆ ☆ ☆ ☆

Quote/s

Personal Review

BOOK REVIEW

Print your book cover and paste it here

Size: 2.5cm x 3cm

Title: _____

Author: _____

Date Started:

Date Finished: _____

Format: Physical   eBook   Audiobook

Rating: ☆☆☆☆☆

Quote/s

Personal Review

BOOK REVIEW

Print your book cover and paste it here

Size: 2.5cm x 3cm

Title: _____

Author: _____

Date Started:

Date Finished:

Format: Physical eBook Audiobook

Rating: ☆☆☆☆☆

Quote/s

Personal Review

BOOK REVIEW

Print your book cover and paste it here

Size: 2.5cm x 3cm

Title: _____

Author: _____

Date Started:

Date Finished: _____

Format: Physical · eBook · Audiobook

Rating: ☆☆☆☆☆

" Quote/s

Personal Review

BOOK REVIEW

Print your book cover and paste it here

Size: 2.5cm x 3cm

Title: _____

Author: _____

Date Started: _____

Date Finished: _____

Format: Physical | eBook | Audiobook

Rating: ☆☆☆☆☆

Quote/s

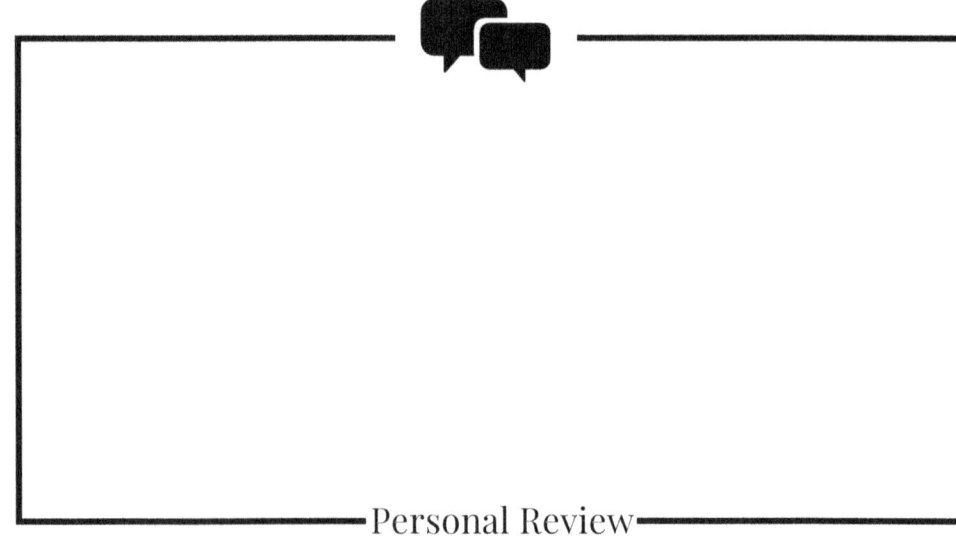

Personal Review

BOOK REVIEW

Print your book cover and paste it here

Size: 2.5cm x 1cm

Title: _____

Author: _____

Date Started:

Date Finished:

Format: Physical   eBook   Audiobook

Rating: ☆☆☆☆☆

Quote/s

Personal Review

BOOK REVIEW

Print your book cover and paste it here

Size: 2.5cm x 1cm

Title: _____

Author: _____

Date Started: _____

Date Finished: _____

Format: Physical   eBook   Audiobook

Rating: ☆☆☆☆☆

" Quote/s

Personal Review

BOOK REVIEW

Print your book cover and paste it here

Size: 2.5cm x 3cm

Title: _____

Author: _____

Date Started: _____

Date Finished: _____

Format: Physical   eBook   Audiobook

Rating: ☆☆☆☆☆

Quote/s

Personal Review

BOOK REVIEW

Print your book cover and paste it here

Size: 2.5cm x 3cm

Title: _____

Author: _____

Date Started: _____

Date Finished: _____

Format: Physical   eBook   Audiobook

Rating: ☆ ☆ ☆ ☆ ☆

Quote/s

Personal Review

BOOK REVIEW

Print your book cover and paste it here

Size: 2.5cm x 3cm

Title: _____

Author: _____

Date Started:

Date Finished:

Format: Physical   eBook   Audiobook

Rating: ☆☆☆☆☆

Quote/s

Personal Review

BOOK REVIEW

Print your book cover and paste it here

Size: 2.5cm x 3cm

Title: _____

Author: _____

Date Started: _____

Date Finished: _____

Format: Physical | eBook | Audiobook

Rating: ☆☆☆☆☆

Quote/s

Personal Review

BOOK REVIEW

Print your book cover and paste it here

Size: 2.5cm x 4cm

Title: _____

Author: _____

Date Started:

Date Finished:

Format: Physical eBook Audiobook

Rating: ☆☆☆☆☆

Quote/s

Personal Review

BOOK REVIEW

Print your book cover and paste it here

Size: 2.5cm x 3cm

Title: _____

Author: _____

Date Started: _____

Date Finished: _____

Format: Physical eBook Audiobook

Rating: ☆☆☆☆☆

" Quote/s

Personal Review

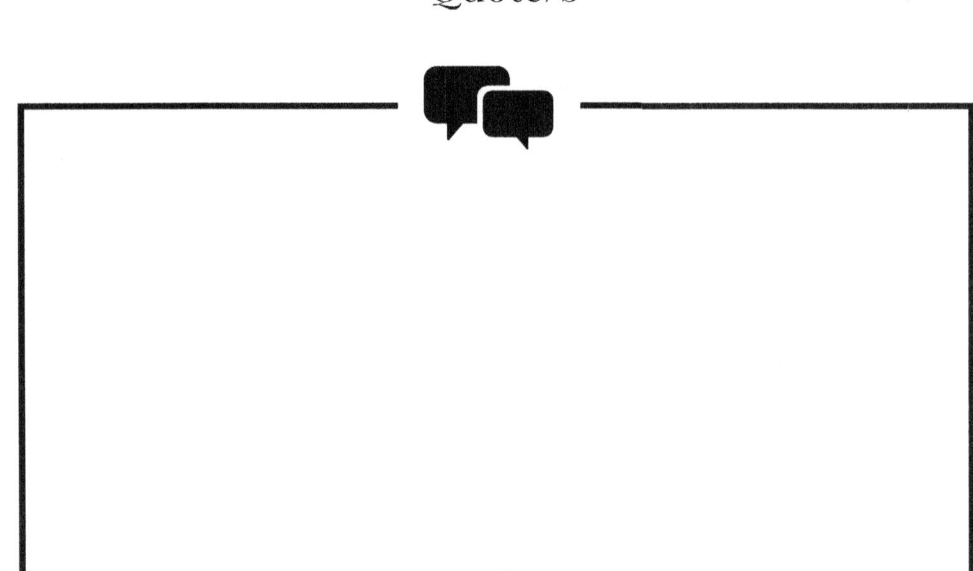

BOOK REVIEW

Print your book cover and paste it here

Size: 2.5cm x 3cm

Title: _____

Author: _____

Date Started:

Date Finished:

Format: Physical eBook Audiobook

Rating: ☆☆☆☆☆

Quote/s

Personal Review

BOOK REVIEW

Print your book cover and paste it here

Size: 2.5cm x 3cm

Title: _____

Author: _____

Date Started: _____

Date Finished: _____

Format: Physical eBook Audiobook

Rating: ☆☆☆☆☆

" Quote/s

Personal Review

BOOK REVIEW

Print your book cover and paste it here

Size: 2.5cm x 3cm

Title: _____

Author: _____

Date Started: _____

Date Finished: _____

Format: Physical   eBook   Audiobook

Rating: ☆ ☆ ☆ ☆ ☆

> ❝
>
>
>
>
>
>
>
>
>
> ## Quote/s

>
>
>
>
>
>
>
>
>
> ## Personal Review

BOOK REVIEW

Print your book cover and paste it here

Size: 2.5cm x 3cm

Title: _____

Author: _____

Date Started: _____

Date Finished: _____

Format: Physical eBook Audiobook

Rating: ☆☆☆☆☆

" Quote/s

💬 Personal Review

BOOK REVIEW

Print your book cover and paste it here

Size: 2.5cm x 4cm

Title: _____

Author: _____

Date Started:

Date Finished:

Format: Physical   eBook   Audiobook

Rating: ☆☆☆☆☆

Quote/s

Personal Review

BOOK REVIEW

Print your book cover and paste it here

Size: 2.5cm x 3cm

Title: _____

Author: _____

Date Started: _____

Date Finished: _____

Format: Physical   eBook   Audiobook

Rating: ☆ ☆ ☆ ☆ ☆

❝

Quote/s

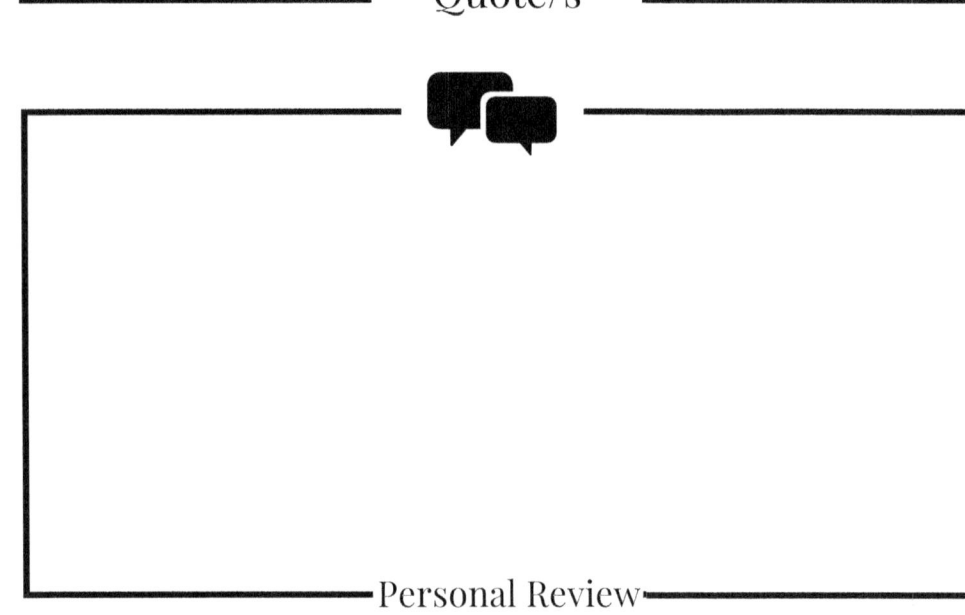

Personal Review

BOOK REVIEW

Print your book cover and paste it here

Size: 2.5cm x 3cm

Title: _____

Author: _____

Date Started: _____

Date Finished: _____

Format: Physical | eBook | Audiobook

Rating: ☆☆☆☆☆

Quote/s

Personal Review

BOOK REVIEW

Print your book cover and paste it here

Size: 2.5cm x 3cm

Title: _____

Author: _____

Date Started:

Date Finished:

Format: Physical   eBook   Audiobook

Rating: ☆☆☆☆☆

Quote/s

Personal Review

BOOK REVIEW

Print your book cover and paste it here

Size: 2.5cm x 3cm

Title: _____

Author: _____

Date Started: _____

Date Finished: _____

Format: Physical   eBook   Audiobook

Rating: ☆☆☆☆☆

" Quote/s

Personal Review

BOOK REVIEW

Print your book cover and paste it here

Size: 2.5cm x 5cm

Title: _____

Author: _____

Date Started:

Date Finished:

Format: Physical   eBook   Audiobook

Rating: ☆☆☆☆☆

Quote/s

Personal Review

BOOK REVIEW

Print your book cover and paste it here

Size: 2.5cm x 3cm

Title: _____

Author: _____

Date Started: _____

Date Finished: _____

Format: Physical   eBook   Audiobook

Rating:  ☆☆☆☆☆

Quote/s

Personal Review

BOOK REVIEW

Print your book cover and paste it here

Size: 2.5cm x 4cm

Title: _____

Author: _____

Date Started:

Date Finished: _____

Format: Physical   eBook   Audiobook

Rating: ☆☆☆☆☆

Quote/s

Personal Review

BOOK REVIEW

Print your book cover and paste it here

Size: 2.5cm x 3cm

Title: _____

Author: _____

Date Started: _____

Date Finished: _____

Format: Physical   eBook   Audiobook

Rating: ☆☆☆☆☆

" Quote/s

Personal Review

BOOK REVIEW

Print your book cover and paste it here

Size: 2.5cm x 3cm

Title: _____

Author: _____

Date Started: _____

Date Finished: _____

Format: Physical   eBook   Audiobook

Rating: ☆☆☆☆☆

Quote/s

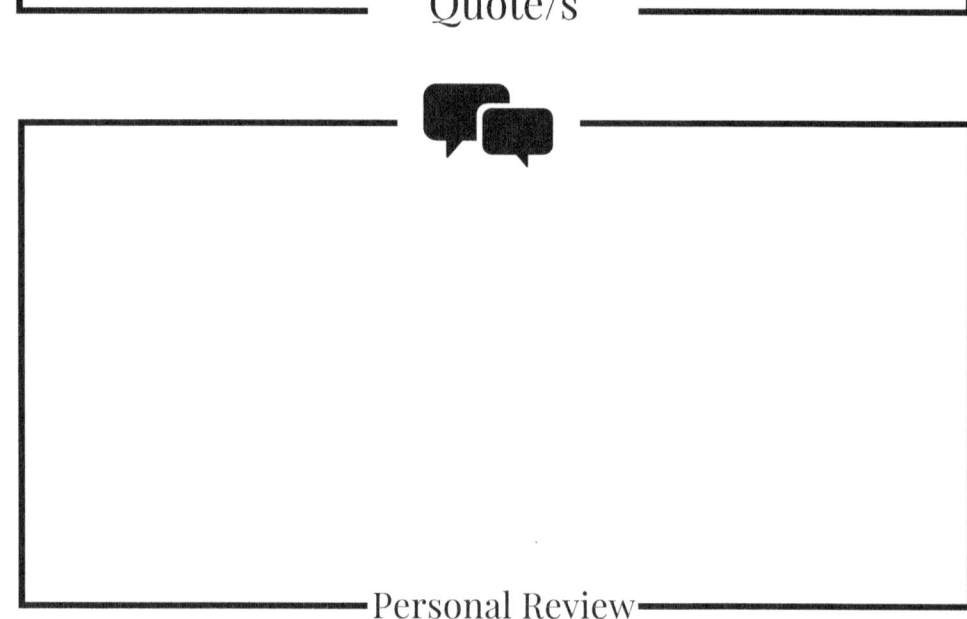

Personal Review

BOOK REVIEW

Print your book cover and paste it here

Size: 2.5cm x 3cm

Title: _____

Author: _____

Date Started:

Date Finished: _____

Format: Physical   eBook   Audiobook

Rating: ☆☆☆☆☆

Quote/s

Personal Review

BOOK REVIEW

Print your book cover and paste it here

Size: 2.5cm x 3cm

Title: _____

Author: _____

Date Started: _____

Date Finished: _____

Format: Physical   eBook   Audiobook

Rating: ☆☆☆☆☆

" Quote/s

Personal Review

BOOK REVIEW

Print your book cover and paste it here

Size: 2.5cm x 3cm

Title: _____

Author: _____

Date Started:

Date Finished:

Format: Physical   eBook   Audiobook

Rating: ☆☆☆☆☆

Quote/s

Personal Review

BOOK REVIEW

Print your book cover and paste it here

Size: 2.5cm x 3cm

Title: _____

Author: _____

Date Started: _____

Date Finished: _____

Format: Physical | eBook | Audiobook

Rating: ☆ ☆ ☆ ☆ ☆

Quote/s

Personal Review

BOOK REVIEW

Print your book cover and paste it here

Size: 2.5cm x 3cm

Title: _____

Author: _____

Date Started:

Date Finished:

Format: Physical   eBook   Audiobook

Rating: ☆☆☆☆☆

Quote/s

Personal Review

BOOK REVIEW

Print your book cover and paste it here

Size: 2.5cm x 3cm

Title: _____

Author: _____

Date Started: _____

Date Finished: _____

Format: Physical   eBook   Audiobook

Rating: ☆☆☆☆☆

" Quote/s

Personal Review

BOOK REVIEW

Print your book cover and paste it here

Size: 2.5cm x 4cm

Title: _____

Author: _____

Date Started: _____

Date Finished: _____

Format: Physical   eBook   Audiobook

Rating: ☆☆☆☆☆

" Quote/s

Personal Review

BOOK REVIEW

Print your book cover and paste it here

Size: 2.5cm x 3cm

Title: _____

Author: _____

Date Started: _____

Date Finished: _____

Format: Physical   eBook   Audiobook

Rating: ☆ ☆ ☆ ☆ ☆

" Quote/s

Personal Review

BOOK REVIEW

Print your book cover and paste it here

Size: 2.5cm x 3cm

Title: _____

Author: _____

Date Started: _____

Date Finished: _____

Format: Physical eBook Audiobook

Rating: ☆☆☆☆☆

Quote/s

Personal Review

BOOK REVIEW

Print your book cover and paste it here

Size: 2.5cm x 3cm

Title: _____

Author: _____

Date Started:

Date Finished:

Format: Physical eBook Audiobook

Rating: ☆ ☆ ☆ ☆ ☆

Quote/s

Personal Review

BOOK REVIEW

Print your book cover and paste it here

Size: 2.5cm x 3cm

Title: _____

Author: _____

Date Started: _____

Date Finished: _____

Format: Physical eBook Audiobook

Rating: ☆☆☆☆☆

Quote/s

Personal Review

BOOK REVIEW

Print your book cover and paste it here

Size: 2.5cm x 3cm

Title: _____

Author: _____

Date Started: _____

Date Finished: _____

Format: Physical eBook Audiobook

Rating: ☆☆☆☆☆

Quote/s

Personal Review

BOOK REVIEW

Print your book cover and paste it here

Size: 2.5cm x 3cm

Title: _____

Author: _____

Date Started:

Date Finished:

Format: Physical eBook Audiobook

Rating: ☆☆☆☆☆

Quote/s

Personal Review

BOOK REVIEW

Print your book cover and paste it here

Size: 2.5cm x 3cm

Title: _____

Author: _____

Date Started: _____

Date Finished: _____

Format: [Physical] [eBook] [Audiobook]

Rating: ☆☆☆☆☆

Quote/s

Personal Review

BOOK REVIEW

Print your book cover and paste it here

Size: 2.5cm x 3cm

Title: _____

Author: _____

Date Started: _____

Date Finished: _____

Format: Physical   eBook   Audiobook

Rating: ☆☆☆☆☆

—— Quote/s ——

—— Personal Review ——

BOOK REVIEW

Print your book cover and paste it here

Size: 2.5cm x 3cm

Title: _____

Author: _____

Date Started:

Date Finished:

Format: Physical   eBook   Audiobook

Rating: ☆☆☆☆☆

Quote/s

Personal Review

BOOK REVIEW

Print your book cover and paste it here

Size: 2.5cm x 3cm

Title: _____

Author: _____

Date Started: _____

Date Finished: _____

Format: Physical   eBook   Audiobook

Rating: ☆☆☆☆☆

" Quote/s

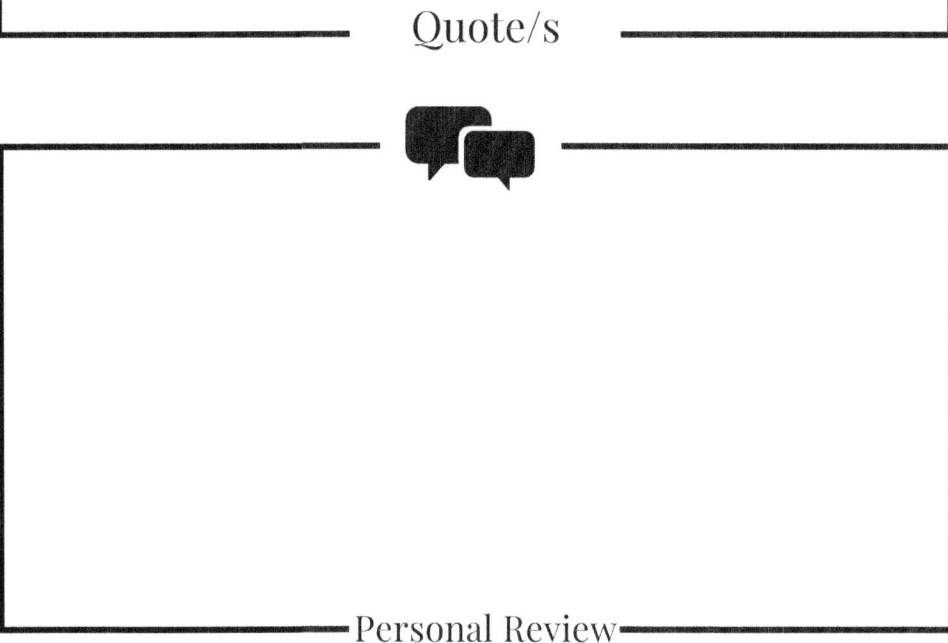

Personal Review

BOOK REVIEW

Print your book cover and paste it here

Size: 2.5cm x 3cm

Title: _____

Author: _____

Date Started: _____

Date Finished: _____

Format: `Physical` `eBook` `Audiobook`

Rating: ☆☆☆☆☆

Quote/s

Personal Review

BOOK REVIEW

Print your book cover and paste it here

Size: 2.5cm x 3cm

Title: _____

Author: _____

Date Started:

Date Finished: _____

Format: Physical eBook Audiobook

Rating: ☆☆☆☆☆

Quote/s

Personal Review

BOOK REVIEW

Print your book cover and paste it here

Size: 2.5cm x 4cm

Title: _____

Author: _____

Date Started:

Date Finished: _____

Format: Physical   eBook   Audiobook

Rating: ☆☆☆☆☆

Quote/s

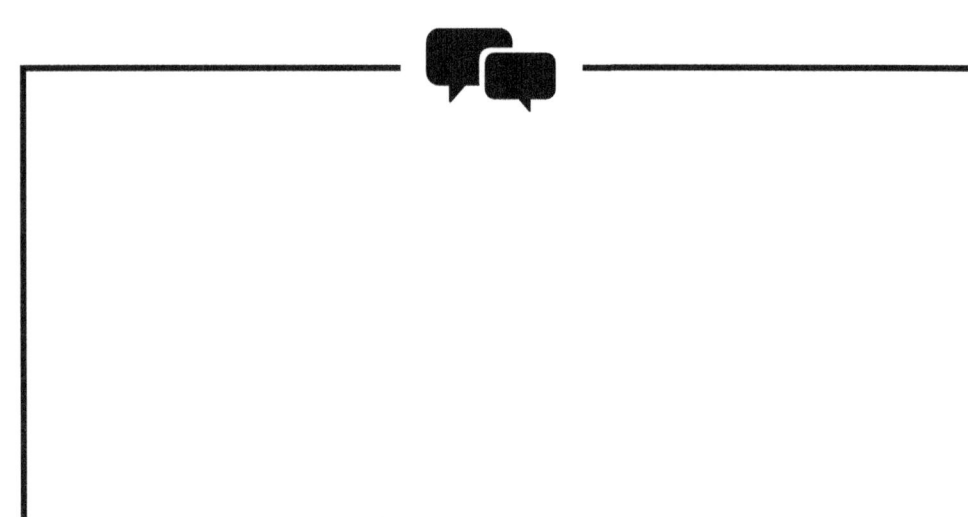

Personal Review

BOOK REVIEW

Print your book cover and paste it here

Size: 2.5cm x 3cm

Title: _____

Author: _____

Date Started:

Date Finished:

Format: Physical eBook Audiobook

Rating: ☆☆☆☆☆

Quote/s

Personal Review

BOOK REVIEW

Print your book cover and paste it here

Size: 2.5cm x 4cm

Title: _____

Author: _____

Date Started: _____

Date Finished: _____

Format: Physical eBook Audiobook

Rating: ☆☆☆☆☆

" Quote/s

Personal Review

BOOK REVIEW

Print your book cover and paste it here

Size: 2.5cm X 3cm

Title: _____

Author: _____

Date Started:

Date Finished: _____

Format: Physical   eBook   Audiobook

Rating: ☆☆☆☆☆

Quote/s

Personal Review

Read 50 Books

Colour in a square when you've finished a book

1	2	3	4	5	6	7	8
9	10	11	12	13	14	15	16
17	18	19	20	21	22	23	24
25	26	27	28	29	30	31	32
33	34	35	36	37	38	39	40
41	42	43	44	45	46	47	48
49	50						

State your genre:

BOOK REVIEW

Print your book cover and paste it here

Size: 2.5cm x 3cm

Title: _____

Author: _____

Date Started:

Date Finished:

Format: Physical   eBook   Audiobook

Rating: ☆☆☆☆☆

Quote/s

Personal Review

BOOK REVIEW

Print your book cover and paste it here

Size: 2.5cm x 3cm

Title: _____

Author: _____

Date Started: _____

Date Finished: _____

Format: Physical | eBook | Audiobook

Rating: ☆☆☆☆☆

Quote/s

Personal Review

BOOK REVIEW

Print your book cover and paste it here

Size: 2.5cm x 4cm

Title: _____

Author: _____

Date Started:

Date Finished:

Format: Physical   eBook   Audiobook

Rating: ☆☆☆☆☆

" Quote/s

Personal Review

BOOK REVIEW

Print your book cover and paste it here

Size: 2.5cm x 3cm

Title: _____

Author: _____

Date Started:

Date Finished: _____

Format: Physical   eBook   Audiobook

Rating: ☆ ☆ ☆ ☆ ☆

Quote/s

Personal Review

BOOK REVIEW

Print your book cover and paste it here

Size: 2.5cm x 3cm

Title: _____

Author: _____

Date Started: _____

Date Finished: _____

Format: Physical   eBook   Audiobook

Rating:  ☆☆☆☆☆

―― Quote/s ――

―― Personal Review ――

BOOK REVIEW

Print your book cover and paste it here

Size: 2.5cm x 3cm

Title: _____

Author: _____

Date Started: _____

Date Finished: _____

Format: Physical eBook Audiobook

Rating: ☆☆☆☆☆

Quote/s

Personal Review

BOOK REVIEW

Print your book cover and paste it here

Size: 2.5cm x 3cm

Title: _____

Author: _____

Date Started:

Date Finished: _____

Format: **Physical** **eBook** **Audiobook**

Rating: ☆☆☆☆☆

Quote/s

Personal Review

BOOK REVIEW

Print your book cover and paste it here

Size: 2.5cm x 4cm

Title: _____

Author: _____

Date Started: _____

Date Finished: _____

Format: Physical eBook Audiobook

Rating: ☆☆☆☆☆

Quote/s

Personal Review

BOOK REVIEW

Print your book cover and paste it here

Size: 2.5cm x 4cm

Title: _____

Author: _____

Date Started:

Date Finished:

Format: Physical eBook Audiobook

Rating: ☆☆☆☆☆

Quote/s

Personal Review

BOOK REVIEW

Print your book cover and paste it here

Size: 2.5cm x 1cm

Title: _____

Author: _____

Date Started: _____

Date Finished: _____

Format: Physical eBook Audiobook

Rating: ☆ ☆ ☆ ☆ ☆

Quote/s

Personal Review

BOOK REVIEW

Print your book cover and paste it here

Size: 2.5cm x 3cm

Title: _____

Author: _____

Date Started: _____

Date Finished: _____

Format: Physical eBook Audiobook

Rating: ☆☆☆☆☆

―― 66 ――

Quote/s

Personal Review

BOOK REVIEW

Print your book cover and paste it here

Size: 2.5cm x 3cm

Title: _____

Author: _____

Date Started: _____

Date Finished: _____

Format: Physical   eBook   Audiobook

Rating: ☆☆☆☆☆

Quote/s

Personal Review

BOOK REVIEW

Print your book cover and paste it here

Size: 2.5cm x 3cm

Title: _____

Author: _____

Date Started:

Date Finished:

Format: Physical   eBook   Audiobook

Rating: ☆☆☆☆☆

" Quote/s

💬 Personal Review

BOOK REVIEW

Print your book cover and paste it here

Size: 2.5cm x 3cm

Title: _____

Author: _____

Date Started: _____

Date Finished: _____

Format: Physical | eBook | Audiobook

Rating: ☆☆☆☆☆

Quote/s

Personal Review

BOOK REVIEW

Print your book cover and paste it here

Size: 2.5cm x 3cm

Title: _____

Author: _____

Date Started: _____

Date Finished: _____

Format: Physical   eBook   Audiobook

Rating: ☆☆☆☆☆

" Quote/s

Personal Review

BOOK REVIEW

Print your book cover and paste it here

Size: 2.5cm x 3cm

Title: _____

Author: _____

Date Started:

Date Finished:

Format: Physical | eBook | Audiobook

Rating: ☆ ☆ ☆ ☆ ☆

Quote/s

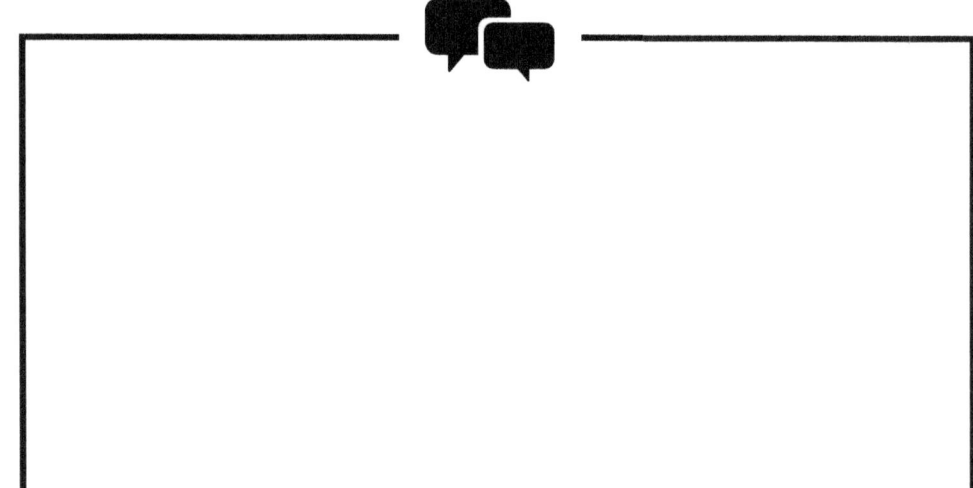

Personal Review

BOOK REVIEW

Print your book cover and paste it here

Size: 2.5cm x 3cm

Title: _____

Author: _____

Date Started: _____

Date Finished: _____

Format: Physical eBook Audiobook

Rating: ☆☆☆☆☆

" Quote/s

Personal Review

BOOK REVIEW

Print your book cover and paste it here

Size: 2.5cm x 3cm

Title: _____

Author: _____

Date Started: _____

Date Finished: _____

Format: `Physical` `eBook` `Audiobook`

Rating: ☆☆☆☆☆

— Quote/s —

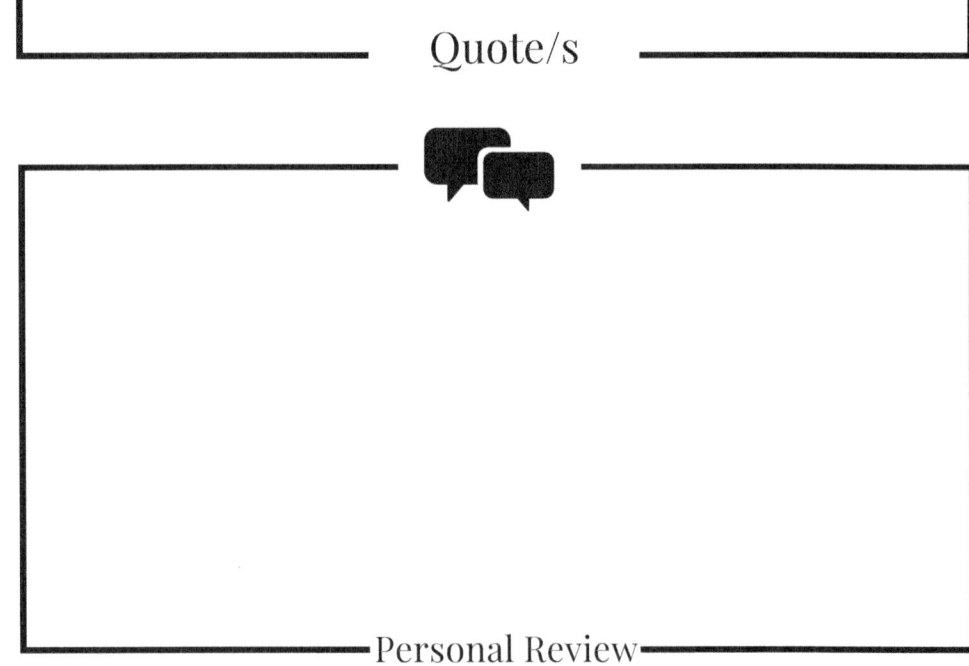

— Personal Review —

BOOK REVIEW

Print your book cover and paste it here

Size: 2.5cm x 3cm

Title: _____

Author: _____

Date Started: _____

Date Finished: _____

Format: Physical eBook Audiobook

Rating: ☆☆☆☆☆

———— 66 ————

Quote/s

Personal Review

BOOK REVIEW

Print your book cover and paste it here

Size: 2.5cm x 3cm

Title: _____

Author: _____

Date Started:

Date Finished:

Format: `Physical` `eBook` `Audiobook`

Rating: ☆☆☆☆☆

" Quote/s

Personal Review

BOOK REVIEW

Print your book cover and paste it here

Size: 2.5cm x 4cm

Title: _____

Author: _____

Date Started:

Date Finished:

Format: Physical   eBook   Audiobook

Rating: ☆☆☆☆☆

Quote/s

Personal Review

BOOK REVIEW

Print your book cover and paste it here

Size: 2.5cm x 4cm

Title: _____

Author: _____

Date Started: _____

Date Finished: _____

Format: Physical   eBook   Audiobook

Rating: ☆☆☆☆☆

" Quote/s

Personal Review

BOOK REVIEW

Print your book cover and paste it here

Size: 2.5cm x 3cm

Title: _____

Author: _____

Date Started: _____

Date Finished: _____

Format: Physical   eBook   Audiobook

Rating: ☆☆☆☆☆

❝ Quote/s

Personal Review

BOOK REVIEW

Print your book cover and paste it here

Size: 2.5cm x 3cm

Title: _____

Author: _____

Date Started: _____

Date Finished: _____

Format: Physical eBook Audiobook

Rating: ☆☆☆☆☆

Quote/s

Personal Review

BOOK REVIEW

Print your book cover and paste it here

Size: 2.5cm x 3cm

Title: _____
Author: _____

Date Started: _____
Date Finished: _____

Format: Physical eBook Audiobook

Rating: ☆☆☆☆☆

" Quote/s

Personal Review

BOOK REVIEW

Print your book cover and paste it here

Size: 2.5cm x 3cm

Title: _____

Author: _____

Date Started: _____

Date Finished: _____

Format: Physical   eBook   Audiobook

Rating: ☆☆☆☆☆

" Quote/s

Personal Review

BOOK REVIEW

Print your book cover and paste it here

Size: 2.5cm x 3cm

Title: _____

Author: _____

Date Started:

Date Finished:

Format: Physical   eBook   Audiobook

Rating: ☆☆☆☆☆

Quote/s

Personal Review

BOOK REVIEW

Print your book cover and paste it here

Size: 2.5cm x 3cm

Title: _____

Author: _____

Date Started:

Date Finished: _____

Format: Physical　eBook　Audiobook

Rating: ☆☆☆☆☆

Quote/s

Personal Review

BOOK REVIEW

Print your book cover and paste it here

Size: 2.5cm x 3cm

Title: _____

Author: _____

Date Started: _____

Date Finished: _____

Format: Physical | eBook | Audiobook

Rating: ☆☆☆☆☆

" Quote/s

💬 Personal Review

BOOK REVIEW

Print your book cover and paste it here

Size: 2.5cm x 3cm

Title: _____

Author: _____

Date Started: _____

Date Finished: _____

Format: Physical | eBook | Audiobook

Rating: ☆☆☆☆☆

Quote/s

Personal Review

BOOK REVIEW

Print your book cover and paste it here

Size: 2.5cm x 3cm

Title: _____

Author: _____

Date Started: _____

Date Finished: _____

Format: Physical   eBook   Audiobook

Rating: ☆☆☆☆☆

Quote/s

Personal Review

BOOK REVIEW

Print your book cover and paste it here

Size: 2.5cm x 3cm

Title: _____

Author: _____

Format: Physical   eBook   Audiobook

Date Started: _____

Date Finished: _____

Rating: ☆☆☆☆☆

" Quote/s

Personal Review

BOOK REVIEW

Print your book cover and paste it here

Size: 2.5cm x 4cm

Title: _____

Author: _____

Date Started:

Date Finished:

Format: Physical   eBook   Audiobook

Rating: ☆☆☆☆☆

Quote/s

Personal Review

BOOK REVIEW

Print your book cover and paste it here

Size: 2.5cm x 3cm

Title: _____

Author: _____

Date Started:

Date Finished:

Format: Physical   eBook   Audiobook

Rating: ☆ ☆ ☆ ☆ ☆

Quote/s

Personal Review

BOOK REVIEW

Print your book cover and paste it here

Size: 2.5cm x 3cm

Title: _____

Author: _____

Date Started: _____

Date Finished: _____

Format: Physical eBook Audiobook

Rating: ☆☆☆☆☆

" Quote/s

Personal Review

BOOK REVIEW

Print your book cover and paste it here

Size: 2.5cm x 3cm

Title: _____

Author: _____

Date Started: _____

Date Finished: _____

Format: Physical | eBook | Audiobook

Rating: ☆☆☆☆☆

Quote/s

Personal Review

BOOK REVIEW

Print your book cover and paste it here

Size: 2.5cm x 3cm

Title: _____

Author: _____

Date Started: _____

Date Finished: _____

Format: Physical eBook Audiobook

Rating: ☆☆☆☆☆

Quote/s

Personal Review

BOOK REVIEW

Print your book cover and paste it here

Size: 2.5cm x 3cm

Title: _____

Author: _____

Date Started:

Date Finished:

Format: `Physical` `eBook` `Audiobook`

Rating: ☆☆☆☆☆

Quote/s

Personal Review

BOOK REVIEW

Print your book cover and paste it here

Size: 2.5cm x 1cm

Title: _____

Author: _____

Date Started:

Date Finished: _____

Format: Physical   eBook   Audiobook

Rating: ☆☆☆☆☆

" Quote/s

💬 Personal Review

BOOK REVIEW

Print your book cover and paste it here

Size: 2.5cm x 3cm

Title: _____

Author: _____

Date Started:

Date Finished:

Format: Physical   eBook   Audiobook

Rating: ☆☆☆☆☆

Quote/s

Personal Review

BOOK REVIEW

Print your book cover and paste it here

Size: 2.5cm x 3cm

Title: _____

Author: _____

Date Started: _____

Date Finished: _____

Format: Physical   eBook   Audiobook

Rating: ☆☆☆☆☆

Quote/s

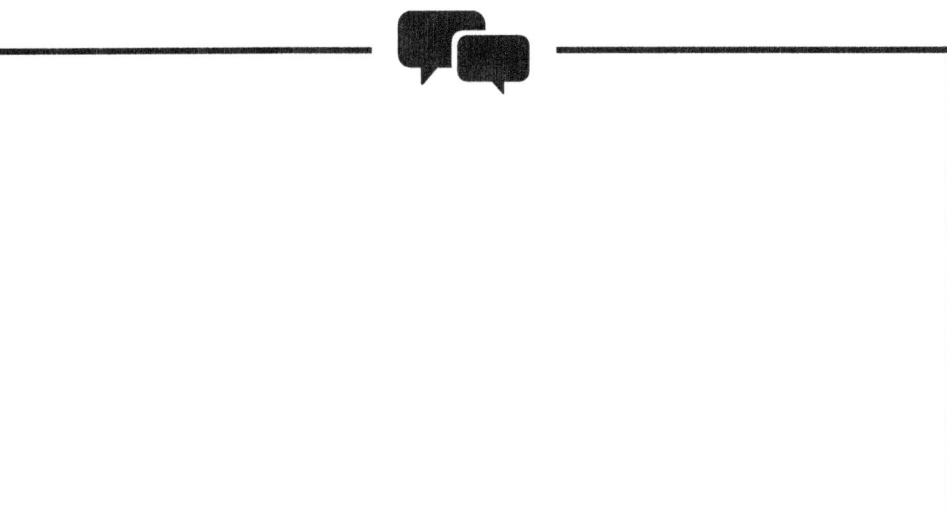

Personal Review

BOOK REVIEW

Print your book cover and paste it here

Size: 2.5cm x 3cm

Title: _____

Author: _____

Date Started: _____

Date Finished: _____

Format: Physical eBook Audiobook

Rating: ☆☆☆☆☆

Quote/s

Personal Review

BOOK REVIEW

Print your book cover and paste it here

Size: 2.5cm x 3cm

Title: _____

Author: _____

Date Started:

Date Finished: _____

Format: Physical eBook Audiobook

Rating: ☆☆☆☆☆

Quote/s

Personal Review

BOOK REVIEW

Print your book cover and paste it here

Size: 2.5cm x 3cm

Title: _____

Author: _____

Date Started: _____

Date Finished: _____

Format: Physical   eBook   Audiobook

Rating: ☆ ☆ ☆ ☆ ☆

❝

Quote/s

Personal Review

BOOK REVIEW

Print your book cover and paste it here

Size: 2.5cm x 3cm

Title: _____

Author: _____

Date Started:

Date Finished:

Format: Physical eBook Audiobook

Rating: ☆☆☆☆☆

Quote/s

Personal Review

BOOK REVIEW

Print your book cover and paste it here

Size: 2.5cm x 3cm

Title: _____

Author: _____

Date Started:

Date Finished:

Format: Physical   eBook   Audiobook

Rating: ☆☆☆☆☆

Quote/s

Personal Review

BOOK REVIEW

Print your book cover and paste it here

Size: 2.5cm x 3cm

Title: _____

Author: _____

Date Started: _____

Date Finished: _____

Format: Physical | eBook | Audiobook

Rating: ☆☆☆☆☆

Quote/s

Personal Review

BOOK REVIEW

Print your book cover and paste it here

Size: 2.5cm x 3cm

Title: _____

Author: _____

Date Started: _____

Date Finished: _____

Format: | Physical | eBook | Audiobook |

Rating: ☆☆☆☆☆

Quote/s

Personal Review

BOOK REVIEW

Print your book cover and paste it here

Size: 2.5cm x 3cm

Title: _____

Author: _____

Date Started: _____

Date Finished: _____

Format: Physical   eBook   Audiobook

Rating: ☆☆☆☆☆

Quote/s

Personal Review

BOOK REVIEW

Print your book cover and paste it here

Size: 2.5cm x 3cm

Title: _____

Author: _____

Date Started: _____

Date Finished: _____

Format: Physical   eBook   Audiobook

Rating: ☆☆☆☆☆

" Quote/s

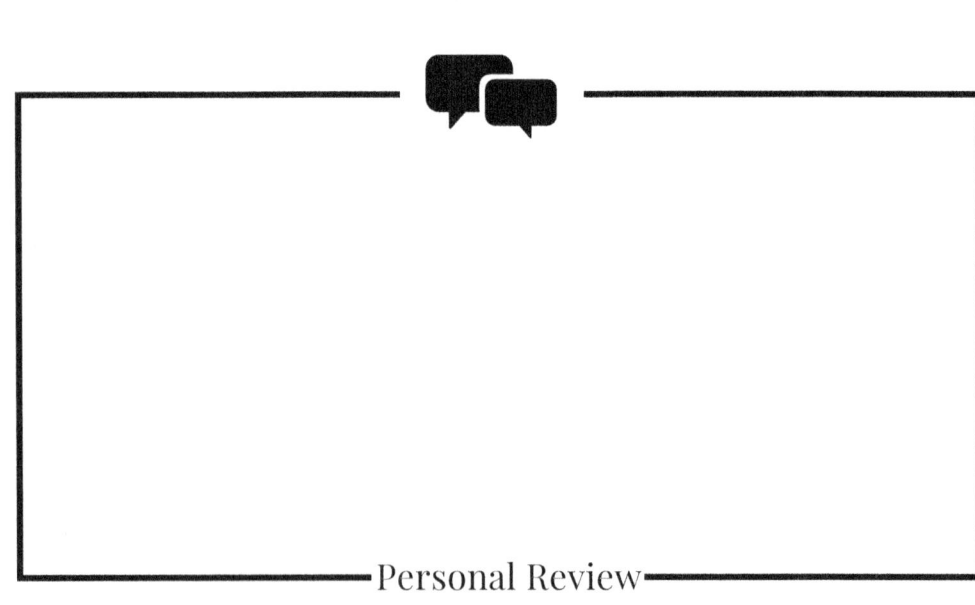

Personal Review

You've read 100 books...

Well done, what an achievement!

Share your completed log book so I can virtually celebrate with you by tagging me online @JenLGilmour.

What will your next 100 books look like?

Notes
A place for your thoughts and scribbles

ABOUT JENNIFER GILMOUR

Jennifer Gilmour is an author and advocate for women in abusive relationships, using her own experiences of domestic abuse as a catalyst to bring awareness and to help others. Jennifer has published two publications, Isolation Junction and Clipped Wings which have both been Amazon Best Sellers and received awards. Jennifer speaks at events across the UK and continues to raise awareness through her blog posts, public speaking, radio interviews and social media.

Most Informative Blogger Award 2018 (Bloggers Bash Annual Awards)
UK & European Award for using Social Media for Good 2019 (Social Day: Social Media Marketing Awards)

Jennifer says: "Together we are Louder".

JenniferGilmour.com
@JenLGilmour

ALSO BY JENNIFER GILMOUR

Isolation Junction

100 reasons to leave, 1,000 reasons to stay

When Rose married the love of her life she was expecting the perfect family life she'd always dreamed of, but before her first child was born her husband, Darren, changed.

Almost overnight Rose's life is turned upside down and the life she'd envisioned seemed like an impossible dream.

As Darren's abuse deepens, Rose has 100 reasons to leave but 1,000s why she can't. Will she ever escape the hellish life she and her children are trapped in?

Can Rose stop her life spiralling further out of control? Can she find the life she desperately wants for her children? Stuck at Isolation Junction, which way will Rose turn?

ALSO BY JENNIFER GILMOUR

Clipped Wings
The silent chorus

Just imagine you thought that you had met the man or woman of your dreams. This person was charming and you thought they were the one or perhaps that this was fate; it was just meant to be.

But as the months go by things start to change. Their behaviour towards you isn't the same, they are more critical, more particular about your appearance, what you do, how you do it, who you see. Months and years go by and you feel isolated from your friends and family because that behaviour has now turned into threats, maybe violence and you feel that your identity is all but gone. But still you stay. Where would you go? Who would help you?

The message of this book is one of courage, as with courage comes awareness and an ability to look back on your relationship and see signs you didn't see before, signs which signify unpleasantness, manipulation, and control.

A group of survivors have written, or been interviewed, about their own experiences. These accounts – in their own words – show that survivors do have a voice and that it needs to be heard. They show that abuse isn't unique or strange but that it is, in fact, a surprisingly common problem in today's society. With their help, we can reach out to educate people about this insidious behaviour.